50 Seasonal Cooking for the Best Homes

By: Kelly Johnson

Table of Contents

- Spring Vegetable Frittata
- Grilled Asparagus with Lemon
- Roasted Spring Carrots with Honey
- Fresh Strawberry Shortcake
- Chilled Pea Soup
- Spring Herb Pesto
- Rhubarb Compote
- Lemon Garlic Shrimp Salad
- Smoked Salmon Crostini
- Grilled Lemon Chicken Skewers
- Wild Mushroom Risotto
- Roasted Beet Salad with Goat Cheese
- Spring Roll Wraps with Peanut Dipping Sauce
- Strawberry Spinach Salad
- Grilled Sweet Potatoes with Cinnamon
- Zucchini Fritters
- Asparagus and Prosciutto Tart
- Cherry Clafoutis
- Grilled Peach Salad with Burrata

- Fresh Mint Ice Cream
- Summer Gazpacho
- Caprese Salad
- Watermelon Feta Salad
- Grilled Vegetables with Balsamic Glaze
- Summer Corn Chowder
- Peach and Burrata Crostini
- Lemon Cucumber Salad
- Fresh Fruit Sorbet
- Coconut Lime Shrimp Tacos
- Sweet Corn Fritters
- Grilled Burger with Avocado Salsa
- Roasted Tomato Basil Soup
- Herb-Infused Summer Sangria
- Grilled Eggplant Parmesan
- Spicy Watermelon Margarita
- Fall Roasted Squash Soup
- Apple Cinnamon Pancakes
- Pumpkin Risotto
- Pear and Walnut Salad
- Braised Short Ribs with Root Vegetables

- Roasted Brussels Sprouts with Balsamic
- Apple Cider Donuts
- Caramelized Onion and Apple Tart
- Sweet Potato Pie
- Butternut Squash and Sage Ravioli
- Roasted Chicken with Autumn Vegetables
- Cranberry Orange Sauce
- Autumn Spice Cake
- Butternut Squash Soup with Cream
- Mulled Wine with Spices

Spring Vegetable Frittata

Ingredients:

- 6 large eggs
- 1 cup mixed spring vegetables (such as spinach, peas, asparagus, and zucchini)
- 1/2 cup grated cheese (such as feta or goat cheese)
- 1/4 cup milk or cream
- 1 tbsp olive oil
- Salt and pepper, to taste

Instructions:

1. Preheat the oven to **375°F (190°C)**.
2. Heat olive oil in a skillet over medium heat.
3. Add the spring vegetables and sauté for **5-7 minutes**, or until tender.
4. In a bowl, whisk together the eggs, milk, cheese, salt, and pepper.
5. Pour the egg mixture over the vegetables in the skillet.
6. Cook for about **2-3 minutes**, then transfer the skillet to the oven.
7. Bake for **10-15 minutes**, or until the frittata is set and golden on top.
8. Slice and serve warm.

Grilled Asparagus with Lemon

Ingredients:

- 1 bunch asparagus
- 1 tbsp olive oil
- Zest and juice of 1 lemon
- Salt and pepper, to taste
- Fresh parsley, for garnish (optional)

Instructions:

1. Preheat the grill to medium-high heat.
2. Trim the woody ends of the asparagus and toss the spears with olive oil, salt, and pepper.
3. Grill the asparagus for **4-5 minutes**, turning occasionally, until tender and slightly charred.
4. Remove from the grill and drizzle with lemon juice and zest.
5. Garnish with fresh parsley and serve immediately.

Roasted Spring Carrots with Honey

Ingredients:

- 1 lb spring carrots, peeled and halved lengthwise
- 1 tbsp olive oil
- 1 tbsp honey
- 1/2 tsp ground cumin (optional)
- Salt and pepper, to taste

Instructions:

1. Preheat the oven to **400°F (200°C)**.
2. Toss the carrots with olive oil, honey, cumin (if using), salt, and pepper.
3. Spread the carrots out in a single layer on a baking sheet.
4. Roast for **20-25 minutes**, or until tender and caramelized.
5. Serve warm.

Fresh Strawberry Shortcake

Ingredients for Biscuits:

- 2 cups all-purpose flour
- 1/4 cup sugar
- 1 tbsp baking powder
- 1/2 tsp salt
- 1/2 cup unsalted butter, cold and cubed
- 3/4 cup heavy cream

Ingredients for Filling:

- 1 lb fresh strawberries, hulled and sliced
- 2 tbsp sugar
- 1 cup whipped cream (store-bought or homemade)

Instructions:

1. Preheat the oven to **425°F (220°C)**.
2. In a bowl, mix together the flour, sugar, baking powder, and salt.
3. Cut in the cold butter until the mixture resembles coarse crumbs.
4. Add the heavy cream and stir until just combined.
5. Turn the dough onto a floured surface and gently knead until it comes together.
6. Pat the dough into a 1-inch thick round and cut into rounds using a biscuit cutter.
7. Place the biscuits on a baking sheet and bake for **10-12 minutes** until golden brown.
8. Meanwhile, combine the sliced strawberries with sugar and let sit for **15-20 minutes** to macerate.

9. To assemble, split the biscuits in half and layer with whipped cream and strawberries.

10. Serve immediately.

Chilled Pea Soup

Ingredients:

- 1 lb fresh or frozen peas
- 1 small onion, chopped
- 2 tbsp olive oil
- 2 cups vegetable broth
- 1/2 cup fresh mint leaves
- Salt and pepper, to taste
- Crème fraîche, for garnish (optional)

Instructions:

1. Heat olive oil in a pot over medium heat and sauté the onion for **5 minutes**, or until softened.
2. Add the peas and vegetable broth to the pot, bringing it to a boil.
3. Reduce heat and simmer for **5-7 minutes** until the peas are tender.
4. Remove from heat and let cool slightly.
5. Blend the soup with fresh mint leaves until smooth.
6. Chill in the fridge for **1-2 hours**.
7. Serve cold, garnished with a dollop of crème fraîche if desired.

Spring Herb Pesto

Ingredients:

- 1 cup fresh herbs (such as basil, mint, parsley, and chives)
- 1/4 cup pine nuts or walnuts
- 1/4 cup grated Parmesan cheese
- 1/2 cup olive oil
- 2 garlic cloves
- Salt and pepper, to taste

Instructions:

1. In a food processor, combine the herbs, nuts, Parmesan, and garlic.
2. Pulse until finely chopped.
3. With the processor running, slowly add the olive oil until the pesto reaches a smooth consistency.
4. Season with salt and pepper to taste.
5. Serve on pasta, bread, or as a topping for roasted vegetables.

Rhubarb Compote

Ingredients:

- 4 cups rhubarb, chopped
- 1/2 cup sugar
- 1/4 cup water
- 1/2 tsp vanilla extract

Instructions:

1. Combine rhubarb, sugar, and water in a saucepan over medium heat.
2. Simmer for **15-20 minutes**, stirring occasionally, until the rhubarb breaks down and the mixture thickens.
3. Remove from heat and stir in the vanilla extract.
4. Let cool and serve on desserts, yogurt, or toast.

Lemon Garlic Shrimp Salad

Ingredients:

- 1 lb shrimp, peeled and deveined
- 1 tbsp olive oil
- 2 garlic cloves, minced
- Zest and juice of 1 lemon
- 4 cups mixed greens
- 1 cucumber, sliced
- 1/2 cup cherry tomatoes, halved
- Salt and pepper, to taste

Instructions:

1. Heat olive oil in a skillet over medium heat.
2. Add the shrimp and garlic, cooking for **3-4 minutes** per side until the shrimp are pink and opaque.
3. Remove from heat and toss with lemon juice and zest.
4. Arrange the mixed greens, cucumber, and tomatoes in a bowl.
5. Top with the lemon garlic shrimp.
6. Serve immediately.

Smoked Salmon Crostini

Ingredients:

- 1 baguette, sliced into 1/2-inch pieces
- 4 oz smoked salmon
- 8 oz cream cheese, softened
- 1 tbsp fresh dill, chopped
- 1 tbsp capers (optional)
- Lemon wedges, for garnish

Instructions:

1. Preheat the oven to **375°F (190°C)** and toast the baguette slices for **5-7 minutes** until golden and crispy.
2. Spread cream cheese on each toasted crostini.
3. Top with smoked salmon and a sprinkle of fresh dill.
4. Garnish with capers and a squeeze of lemon.
5. Serve immediately.

Grilled Lemon Chicken Skewers

Ingredients:

- 1 lb chicken breast, cut into 1-inch cubes
- 2 tbsp olive oil
- Zest and juice of 2 lemons
- 2 garlic cloves, minced
- 1 tbsp fresh thyme, chopped
- Salt and pepper, to taste
- Wooden skewers, soaked in water for 30 minutes

Instructions:

1. In a bowl, combine olive oil, lemon zest, lemon juice, garlic, thyme, salt, and pepper.
2. Add the chicken cubes and marinate for **30 minutes to 1 hour** in the fridge.
3. Preheat the grill to medium-high heat.
4. Thread the marinated chicken onto the skewers.
5. Grill for **4-5 minutes per side** or until the chicken is cooked through and has grill marks.
6. Serve immediately with your favorite sides.

Wild Mushroom Risotto

Ingredients:

- 1 1/2 cups Arborio rice
- 1 lb wild mushrooms (such as shiitake, oyster, or cremini), sliced
- 1 small onion, chopped
- 3 tbsp butter
- 1/2 cup dry white wine
- 4 cups chicken or vegetable broth, kept warm
- 1/2 cup Parmesan cheese, grated
- Salt and pepper, to taste

Instructions:

1. In a large pan, heat 2 tbsp of butter over medium heat.
2. Add the chopped onion and cook until translucent, about **3-4 minutes**.
3. Add the mushrooms and cook until softened and browned, about **5-7 minutes**.
4. Add the Arborio rice and stir for **2 minutes** to lightly toast the rice.
5. Pour in the white wine and cook until absorbed.
6. Gradually add the warm broth, **1/2 cup at a time**, stirring constantly, allowing each addition to be absorbed before adding more.
7. Continue this process until the rice is tender and creamy, about **20-25 minutes**.
8. Stir in the Parmesan cheese, the remaining butter, salt, and pepper.
9. Serve warm.

Roasted Beet Salad with Goat Cheese

Ingredients:

- 4 medium beets, peeled and cut into wedges
- 2 tbsp olive oil
- Salt and pepper, to taste
- 4 cups mixed greens (arugula, spinach, etc.)
- 1/2 cup goat cheese, crumbled
- 1/4 cup walnuts, toasted
- 1 tbsp balsamic vinegar

Instructions:

1. Preheat the oven to **400°F (200°C)**.
2. Toss the beet wedges in olive oil, salt, and pepper.
3. Arrange the beets on a baking sheet and roast for **25-30 minutes**, flipping halfway through, until tender.
4. Let the beets cool slightly.
5. In a large bowl, toss the mixed greens with the roasted beets, crumbled goat cheese, and toasted walnuts.
6. Drizzle with balsamic vinegar and serve immediately.

Spring Roll Wraps with Peanut Dipping Sauce

Ingredients for Spring Rolls:

- 8 rice paper wraps
- 1 cup cooked shrimp, sliced
- 1 cup shredded carrots
- 1 cucumber, julienned
- 1 cup fresh mint leaves
- 1 cup fresh cilantro leaves
- 1/2 cup cooked vermicelli noodles (optional)

Ingredients for Peanut Dipping Sauce:

- 1/4 cup peanut butter
- 2 tbsp soy sauce
- 1 tbsp honey
- 1 tbsp rice vinegar
- 1 tbsp water
- 1 tsp sesame oil

Instructions:

1. Fill a shallow bowl with warm water. Dip one rice paper wrap into the water for **5 seconds** until soft.
2. Place the softened rice paper on a clean surface.
3. Layer shrimp, carrots, cucumber, herbs, and noodles (if using) in the center of the wrap.
4. Fold in the sides and roll tightly. Repeat for the remaining rolls.

5. For the dipping sauce, whisk together all the ingredients in a bowl until smooth.

6. Serve the spring rolls with the peanut dipping sauce.

Strawberry Spinach Salad

Ingredients:

- 4 cups fresh spinach
- 1 cup strawberries, sliced
- 1/4 cup red onion, thinly sliced
- 1/4 cup feta cheese, crumbled
- 1/4 cup walnuts, toasted

Ingredients for Dressing:

- 2 tbsp balsamic vinegar
- 1 tbsp honey
- 2 tbsp olive oil
- Salt and pepper, to taste

Instructions:

1. In a large bowl, toss the spinach, strawberries, red onion, feta cheese, and walnuts.
2. In a small bowl, whisk together the balsamic vinegar, honey, olive oil, salt, and pepper.
3. Drizzle the dressing over the salad and toss to combine.
4. Serve immediately.

Grilled Sweet Potatoes with Cinnamon

Ingredients:

- 2 large sweet potatoes, peeled and cut into 1/2-inch slices
- 2 tbsp olive oil
- 1/2 tsp ground cinnamon
- Salt and pepper, to taste

Instructions:

1. Preheat the grill to medium heat.
2. Toss the sweet potato slices in olive oil, cinnamon, salt, and pepper.
3. Grill the sweet potatoes for **4-5 minutes per side**, until tender and slightly charred.
4. Serve warm.

Zucchini Fritters

Ingredients:

- 2 medium zucchinis, grated
- 1/2 cup flour
- 2 eggs
- 1/2 cup grated Parmesan cheese
- 1 garlic clove, minced
- Salt and pepper, to taste
- Olive oil for frying

Instructions:

1. Place the grated zucchini in a clean towel and squeeze out any excess moisture.
2. In a bowl, combine the zucchini, flour, eggs, Parmesan, garlic, salt, and pepper.
3. Heat olive oil in a skillet over medium heat.
4. Scoop spoonfuls of the zucchini mixture into the skillet, pressing them down slightly.
5. Fry for **2-3 minutes per side**, until golden brown.
6. Serve warm with sour cream or yogurt.

Asparagus and Prosciutto Tart

Ingredients:

- 1 sheet puff pastry
- 12 asparagus spears, trimmed
- 6 slices prosciutto
- 1/2 cup ricotta cheese
- 1 tbsp olive oil
- Salt and pepper, to taste

Instructions:

1. Preheat the oven to **375°F (190°C)**.
2. Roll out the puff pastry on a baking sheet lined with parchment paper.
3. Spread ricotta cheese evenly over the pastry, leaving a small border around the edges.
4. Arrange the prosciutto slices and asparagus on top of the ricotta.
5. Drizzle with olive oil and season with salt and pepper.
6. Bake for **20-25 minutes** or until the pastry is golden and puffed.
7. Slice and serve warm.

Cherry Clafoutis

Ingredients:

- 2 cups fresh cherries, pitted
- 3/4 cup milk
- 1/2 cup sugar
- 3 eggs
- 1 tsp vanilla extract
- 1/2 cup all-purpose flour
- Powdered sugar, for dusting

Instructions:

1. Preheat the oven to **350°F (175°C)**.
2. Grease a baking dish and arrange the cherries in the bottom.
3. In a bowl, whisk together the milk, sugar, eggs, vanilla, and flour until smooth.
4. Pour the batter over the cherries.
5. Bake for **35-40 minutes** or until set and lightly golden.
6. Dust with powdered sugar and serve warm or at room temperature.

Grilled Peach Salad with Burrata

Ingredients:

- 4 ripe peaches, halved and pitted
- 2 tbsp olive oil
- 4 cups mixed greens (arugula, spinach, etc.)
- 1 ball of burrata cheese, torn into pieces
- 1/4 cup toasted almonds, chopped
- 1 tbsp honey
- 1 tbsp balsamic glaze
- Salt and pepper, to taste

Instructions:

1. Preheat the grill to medium heat.
2. Brush the peach halves with olive oil and grill for **2-3 minutes per side**, until grill marks appear and the peaches soften.
3. In a large bowl, toss the mixed greens.
4. Arrange the grilled peaches, burrata, and toasted almonds on top of the greens.
5. Drizzle with honey and balsamic glaze.
6. Season with salt and pepper and serve immediately.

Fresh Mint Ice Cream

Ingredients:

- 1 cup fresh mint leaves, chopped
- 2 cups heavy cream
- 1 cup whole milk
- 3/4 cup sugar
- 1 tsp vanilla extract
- 1/4 tsp salt
- 4 large egg yolks

Instructions:

1. In a saucepan, heat the milk, heavy cream, sugar, vanilla extract, and salt over medium heat until warm, but not boiling.
2. Add the mint leaves and steep for **15-20 minutes**, then strain out the mint.
3. In a separate bowl, whisk the egg yolks. Slowly add a bit of the warm cream mixture into the egg yolks to temper them, then pour the egg yolk mixture back into the saucepan.
4. Cook on low heat, stirring constantly until the mixture thickens and coats the back of a spoon.
5. Remove from heat, let cool, then chill in the fridge for at least **2 hours**.
6. Once chilled, churn the mixture in an ice cream maker according to the manufacturer's instructions.
7. Transfer to a container and freeze for **4 hours** before serving.

Summer Gazpacho

Ingredients:

- 4 ripe tomatoes, chopped
- 1 cucumber, peeled and chopped
- 1 red bell pepper, chopped
- 1/2 red onion, chopped
- 1 clove garlic, minced
- 1/4 cup olive oil
- 2 tbsp red wine vinegar
- Salt and pepper, to taste
- Fresh basil, for garnish

Instructions:

1. In a blender or food processor, combine the tomatoes, cucumber, bell pepper, onion, and garlic.
2. Blend until smooth, then add the olive oil, red wine vinegar, salt, and pepper.
3. Blend again to combine.
4. Chill in the fridge for **1 hour** before serving.
5. Garnish with fresh basil and serve cold.

Caprese Salad

Ingredients:

- 4 large tomatoes, sliced
- 1 ball of fresh mozzarella cheese, sliced
- Fresh basil leaves
- 2 tbsp olive oil
- 1 tbsp balsamic vinegar
- Salt and pepper, to taste

Instructions:

1. On a platter, alternate slices of tomato, mozzarella, and basil leaves.
2. Drizzle with olive oil and balsamic vinegar.
3. Season with salt and pepper.
4. Serve immediately.

Watermelon Feta Salad

Ingredients:

- 4 cups watermelon, cubed
- 1/2 cup feta cheese, crumbled
- 1/4 cup fresh mint leaves, chopped
- 1 tbsp olive oil
- 1 tbsp lime juice
- Salt and pepper, to taste

Instructions:

1. In a large bowl, combine the watermelon, feta, and mint.
2. Drizzle with olive oil and lime juice.
3. Season with salt and pepper and toss gently.
4. Serve chilled.

Grilled Vegetables with Balsamic Glaze

Ingredients:

- 1 zucchini, sliced
- 1 red bell pepper, sliced
- 1 yellow bell pepper, sliced
- 1 red onion, sliced
- 2 tbsp olive oil
- Salt and pepper, to taste
- 1/4 cup balsamic glaze

Instructions:

1. Preheat the grill to medium heat.
2. Toss the sliced vegetables with olive oil, salt, and pepper.
3. Grill the vegetables for **3-4 minutes per side** until tender and charred.
4. Drizzle with balsamic glaze and serve immediately.

Summer Corn Chowder

Ingredients:

- 4 ears of fresh corn, kernels removed
- 1 tbsp butter
- 1 small onion, chopped
- 1 clove garlic, minced
- 2 cups vegetable or chicken broth
- 1 cup milk
- 1/2 cup cream
- Salt and pepper, to taste
- Fresh parsley, for garnish

Instructions:

1. In a large pot, melt butter over medium heat.
2. Add the onion and garlic and sauté for **3-4 minutes** until softened.
3. Add the corn kernels and broth. Bring to a simmer and cook for **10-15 minutes**.
4. Use an immersion blender to partially blend the chowder, leaving some corn kernels intact for texture.
5. Stir in the milk and cream, and season with salt and pepper.
6. Serve garnished with fresh parsley.

Peach and Burrata Crostini

Ingredients:

- 1 baguette, sliced into 1/2-inch rounds
- 2 tbsp olive oil
- 2 ripe peaches, sliced
- 1 ball burrata cheese
- Fresh basil leaves
- Honey, for drizzling
- Salt and pepper, to taste

Instructions:

1. Preheat the oven to **375°F (190°C)**.
2. Arrange the baguette slices on a baking sheet and brush with olive oil.
3. Toast in the oven for **8-10 minutes**, until golden.
4. Arrange the toasted bread with slices of peach, burrata cheese, and fresh basil.
5. Drizzle with honey, season with salt and pepper, and serve immediately.

Lemon Cucumber Salad

Ingredients:

- 1 cucumber, thinly sliced
- 1/2 red onion, thinly sliced
- 1/4 cup fresh dill, chopped
- 2 tbsp olive oil
- 1 tbsp lemon juice
- Salt and pepper, to taste

Instructions:

1. In a large bowl, combine the cucumber, onion, and dill.
2. Drizzle with olive oil and lemon juice.
3. Season with salt and pepper and toss to combine.
4. Serve immediately or chill for **30 minutes** for the flavors to meld.

Fresh Fruit Sorbet

Ingredients:

- 3 cups fresh fruit (mango, berries, peach, etc.)
- 1/2 cup sugar
- 1 tbsp lemon juice
- 1/4 cup water

Instructions:

1. In a blender, combine the fruit, sugar, lemon juice, and water.
2. Blend until smooth.
3. Pour the mixture into an ice cream maker and churn according to the manufacturer's instructions.
4. Freeze for at least **2 hours** before serving.

Coconut Lime Shrimp Tacos

Ingredients:

- 1 lb shrimp, peeled and deveined
- 1/2 cup shredded coconut
- 1/4 cup breadcrumbs
- 1 tsp lime zest
- 2 tbsp lime juice
- 1 tbsp olive oil
- Salt and pepper, to taste
- Small tortillas
- Shredded lettuce
- Avocado slices
- Fresh cilantro

Instructions:

1. Preheat the oven to **375°F (190°C)**.
2. In a bowl, mix the shredded coconut, breadcrumbs, lime zest, salt, and pepper.
3. Coat the shrimp with the coconut mixture and place them on a baking sheet lined with parchment paper.
4. Drizzle with olive oil and bake for **8-10 minutes**, until shrimp are cooked through and crispy.
5. Warm the tortillas and fill them with the shrimp, lettuce, avocado slices, and fresh cilantro.
6. Drizzle with lime juice and serve.

Sweet Corn Fritters

Ingredients:

- 2 cups fresh corn kernels (or canned/frozen)
- 1/2 cup all-purpose flour
- 1/4 cup cornmeal
- 1 tsp baking powder
- 1/2 tsp salt
- 1/4 tsp black pepper
- 1/4 cup milk
- 1 large egg
- 2 tbsp chopped green onions
- 2 tbsp fresh cilantro, chopped
- Vegetable oil, for frying

Instructions:

1. In a bowl, combine flour, cornmeal, baking powder, salt, and pepper.
2. In another bowl, whisk the egg and milk together.
3. Add the wet ingredients to the dry ingredients and stir to combine.
4. Fold in the corn, green onions, and cilantro.
5. Heat vegetable oil in a skillet over medium-high heat.
6. Drop spoonfuls of the corn mixture into the hot oil and fry until golden brown, **2-3 minutes per side**.
7. Drain on paper towels and serve hot.

Grilled Burger with Avocado Salsa

Ingredients:

- 1 lb ground beef (or turkey)
- Salt and pepper, to taste
- 4 burger buns
- 1 avocado, diced
- 1/2 cup diced tomatoes
- 1/4 cup red onion, finely chopped
- 1 tbsp lime juice
- 1 tbsp chopped cilantro

Instructions:

1. Preheat the grill to medium-high heat.
2. Season the ground beef with salt and pepper and shape into 4 patties.
3. Grill the patties for **4-5 minutes per side** until desired doneness.
4. While grilling, mix the avocado, tomatoes, red onion, lime juice, cilantro, and salt in a bowl to make the salsa.
5. Toast the burger buns on the grill for 1-2 minutes.
6. Assemble the burgers by placing the patties on the buns and topping with the avocado salsa. Serve immediately.

Roasted Tomato Basil Soup

Ingredients:

- 6 large tomatoes, halved
- 1 onion, quartered
- 3 cloves garlic, peeled
- 2 tbsp olive oil
- Salt and pepper, to taste
- 2 cups vegetable broth
- 1/4 cup fresh basil, chopped
- 1/2 cup heavy cream (optional)

Instructions:

1. Preheat the oven to **400°F (200°C)**.
2. Place the tomatoes, onion, and garlic on a baking sheet, drizzle with olive oil, and season with salt and pepper.
3. Roast for **25-30 minutes** until the tomatoes are soft and caramelized.
4. Transfer the roasted vegetables to a blender and blend until smooth.
5. Pour the blended mixture into a pot, add the vegetable broth, and simmer over low heat for **10 minutes**.
6. Stir in the fresh basil and heavy cream (if using), and serve.

Herb-Infused Summer Sangria

Ingredients:

- 1 bottle white wine (such as Sauvignon Blanc)
- 1/4 cup brandy
- 1/4 cup honey or simple syrup
- 1 orange, thinly sliced
- 1 lemon, thinly sliced
- 1 lime, thinly sliced
- 1/2 cup fresh mint leaves
- 1/2 cup fresh basil leaves
- 1/2 cup soda water or club soda (optional)

Instructions:

1. In a large pitcher, combine the wine, brandy, and honey or simple syrup.
2. Add the sliced fruit, mint, and basil. Stir to combine.
3. Cover and refrigerate for at least **4 hours** (overnight for best flavor).
4. Before serving, add soda water or club soda for a fizzy touch, if desired.
5. Serve over ice with extra mint and basil leaves for garnish.

Grilled Eggplant Parmesan

Ingredients:

- 2 large eggplants, sliced into 1/2-inch thick rounds
- 1/4 cup olive oil
- Salt and pepper, to taste
- 2 cups marinara sauce
- 1 1/2 cups shredded mozzarella cheese
- 1/2 cup grated Parmesan cheese
- Fresh basil leaves, for garnish

Instructions:

1. Preheat the grill to medium-high heat.
2. Brush the eggplant slices with olive oil and season with salt and pepper.
3. Grill the eggplant slices for **3-4 minutes per side**, until tender and grill marks appear.
4. Preheat the oven to **375°F (190°C)**.
5. In a baking dish, layer the grilled eggplant, marinara sauce, mozzarella, and Parmesan cheese.
6. Repeat the layers, finishing with a layer of cheese.
7. Bake for **15-20 minutes** until the cheese is melted and bubbly.
8. Garnish with fresh basil and serve.

Spicy Watermelon Margarita

Ingredients:

- 2 cups watermelon, cubed
- 2 oz tequila
- 1 oz lime juice
- 1 oz triple sec
- 1/2 oz agave syrup (or simple syrup)
- 1-2 slices jalapeño pepper
- Salt, for rim (optional)
- Lime wedge, for garnish

Instructions:

1. In a blender, combine the watermelon, tequila, lime juice, triple sec, agave syrup, and jalapeño.
2. Blend until smooth.
3. Rim the glass with salt (optional) and pour the watermelon mixture into the glass.
4. Garnish with a lime wedge and serve chilled.

Fall Roasted Squash Soup

Ingredients:

- 1 medium butternut squash, peeled and cubed
- 1 onion, chopped
- 2 cloves garlic, minced
- 4 cups vegetable or chicken broth
- 1/2 tsp ground cinnamon
- 1/4 tsp ground nutmeg
- Salt and pepper, to taste
- 1/2 cup heavy cream (optional)

Instructions:

1. Preheat the oven to **400°F (200°C)**.
2. Toss the squash with olive oil, salt, and pepper, and roast for **25-30 minutes** until tender.
3. In a large pot, sauté the onion and garlic in olive oil over medium heat until softened, about **5 minutes**.
4. Add the roasted squash, broth, cinnamon, and nutmeg, and bring to a simmer.
5. Blend the soup using an immersion blender until smooth.
6. Stir in the heavy cream (if using) and adjust the seasoning with salt and pepper.
7. Serve hot.

Apple Cinnamon Pancakes

Ingredients:

- 1 1/2 cups all-purpose flour
- 1 tbsp sugar
- 2 tsp baking powder
- 1/2 tsp cinnamon
- 1/4 tsp salt
- 1 cup milk
- 1 large egg
- 2 tbsp melted butter
- 1 apple, peeled and diced
- Maple syrup, for serving

Instructions:

1. In a bowl, whisk together the flour, sugar, baking powder, cinnamon, and salt.
2. In another bowl, whisk the milk, egg, and melted butter together.
3. Add the wet ingredients to the dry ingredients and stir until just combined.
4. Fold in the diced apple.
5. Heat a non-stick skillet over medium heat and lightly grease with butter or oil.
6. Pour 1/4 cup of batter onto the skillet for each pancake and cook until bubbles form on the surface, about **2-3 minutes**.
7. Flip the pancakes and cook for an additional **1-2 minutes** until golden brown.
8. Serve with maple syrup.

Pumpkin Risotto

Ingredients:

- 1 cup Arborio rice
- 2 tbsp olive oil
- 1 small onion, finely chopped
- 2 cloves garlic, minced
- 1 1/2 cups pumpkin puree
- 4 cups chicken or vegetable broth, kept warm
- 1/2 cup dry white wine
- 1/2 cup grated Parmesan cheese
- 2 tbsp butter
- Salt and pepper, to taste
- Fresh sage leaves, for garnish (optional)

Instructions:

1. In a large pot, heat olive oil over medium heat. Add the onion and garlic and sauté until softened, about **3-4 minutes**.

2. Add the Arborio rice and cook, stirring, for about **1-2 minutes** until the rice is lightly toasted.

3. Pour in the white wine and cook until it's absorbed, about **2 minutes**.

4. Gradually add the warm broth, about 1/2 cup at a time, stirring frequently. Allow the liquid to be absorbed before adding more.

5. When the rice is almost tender (about **18-20 minutes**), stir in the pumpkin puree, Parmesan cheese, and butter.

6. Season with salt and pepper to taste, and cook for an additional **2-3 minutes** until creamy.

7. Garnish with fresh sage and serve.

Pear and Walnut Salad

Ingredients:

- 2 ripe pears, sliced
- 1/2 cup walnuts, toasted
- 4 cups mixed greens (arugula, spinach, etc.)
- 1/4 cup crumbled blue cheese (optional)
- 1/4 cup balsamic vinaigrette dressing
- 1 tbsp honey
- Salt and pepper, to taste

Instructions:

1. In a large bowl, toss the mixed greens with the balsamic vinaigrette and honey.
2. Add the sliced pears and toasted walnuts to the salad and toss gently.
3. Top with crumbled blue cheese, if desired, and season with salt and pepper.
4. Serve immediately.

Braised Short Ribs with Root Vegetables

Ingredients:

- 4 beef short ribs
- 2 tbsp olive oil
- Salt and pepper, to taste
- 1 onion, chopped
- 2 carrots, peeled and chopped
- 2 celery stalks, chopped
- 4 cloves garlic, minced
- 2 cups red wine
- 2 cups beef broth
- 2 sprigs thyme
- 2 sprigs rosemary
- 2 bay leaves
- 3 potatoes, peeled and cubed
- 1/2 cup heavy cream (optional)

Instructions:

1. Preheat the oven to **350°F (175°C)**.

2. Heat olive oil in a large ovenproof pot over medium-high heat. Season the short ribs with salt and pepper, and brown them on all sides, about **5-7 minutes**.

3. Remove the ribs and set aside. In the same pot, sauté the onion, carrots, celery, and garlic until softened, about **5 minutes**.

4. Add the wine and beef broth, scraping up any browned bits from the bottom of the pot.

5. Return the short ribs to the pot and add the thyme, rosemary, and bay leaves. Bring to a simmer.

6. Cover the pot and transfer it to the oven. Braise for **2 1/2 to 3 hours** until the meat is tender.

7. Add the potatoes to the pot during the last **30 minutes** of cooking.

8. After the short ribs are done, remove the ribs and vegetables from the pot. If desired, stir in heavy cream to make the sauce creamy.

9. Serve the short ribs with the vegetables and sauce.

Roasted Brussels Sprouts with Balsamic

Ingredients:

- 1 lb Brussels sprouts, trimmed and halved
- 2 tbsp olive oil
- 1 tbsp balsamic vinegar
- Salt and pepper, to taste
- 1 tbsp honey (optional)

Instructions:

1. Preheat the oven to **400°F (200°C)**.
2. Toss the Brussels sprouts with olive oil, balsamic vinegar, salt, and pepper.
3. Spread the sprouts on a baking sheet in a single layer.
4. Roast for **20-25 minutes**, shaking the pan halfway through, until crispy and golden brown.
5. Drizzle with honey (if using) before serving.

Apple Cider Donuts

Ingredients:

- 2 cups all-purpose flour
- 1 1/2 tsp baking powder
- 1/2 tsp baking soda
- 1 tsp ground cinnamon
- 1/2 tsp ground nutmeg
- 1/2 tsp salt
- 1/2 cup granulated sugar
- 1/4 cup brown sugar
- 2 large eggs
- 1/2 cup apple cider
- 1/4 cup milk
- 1/4 cup melted butter
- 1 tsp vanilla extract
- Vegetable oil for frying
- Cinnamon sugar for coating

Instructions:

1. In a bowl, whisk together the flour, baking powder, baking soda, cinnamon, nutmeg, and salt.

2. In a separate bowl, whisk together the granulated sugar, brown sugar, eggs, apple cider, milk, melted butter, and vanilla extract.

3. Add the wet ingredients to the dry ingredients and stir until just combined.

4. Heat the oil in a deep fryer or large pot to **350°F (175°C)**.

5. Carefully spoon the donut batter into a piping bag or a zip-top bag with the tip cut off.

6. Pipe the batter into the hot oil, making 2-inch rounds. Fry for **2-3 minutes** per side until golden brown.

7. Drain on paper towels and toss in cinnamon sugar while still warm. Serve.

Caramelized Onion and Apple Tart

Ingredients:

- 1 sheet puff pastry, thawed
- 2 medium onions, thinly sliced
- 1 tbsp olive oil
- 1 tbsp butter
- 1 apple, thinly sliced
- 1/2 tsp thyme
- 1/4 cup grated Gruyère cheese
- Salt and pepper, to taste

Instructions:

1. Preheat the oven to **375°F (190°C)**.
2. In a skillet, heat olive oil and butter over medium heat. Add the onions and cook, stirring frequently, until caramelized, about **20-25 minutes**.
3. Season with salt, pepper, and thyme, then set aside.
4. Roll out the puff pastry on a baking sheet and score a 1-inch border around the edges.
5. Spread the caramelized onions evenly over the pastry. Arrange the apple slices on top and sprinkle with Gruyère cheese.
6. Bake for **20-25 minutes** until the pastry is golden brown and crispy.
7. Slice and serve warm.

Sweet Potato Pie

Ingredients:

- 2 cups cooked and mashed sweet potatoes
- 3/4 cup granulated sugar
- 1/2 cup brown sugar
- 2 large eggs
- 1/2 cup evaporated milk
- 1/2 tsp ground cinnamon
- 1/4 tsp ground nutmeg
- 1/4 tsp ground ginger
- 1/2 tsp vanilla extract
- 1/4 tsp salt
- 1 prepared pie crust

Instructions:

1. Preheat the oven to **350°F (175°C)**.
2. In a large bowl, combine the mashed sweet potatoes, granulated sugar, brown sugar, eggs, evaporated milk, cinnamon, nutmeg, ginger, vanilla, and salt.
3. Mix until smooth and well-combined.
4. Pour the mixture into the pie crust and smooth the top.
5. Bake for **45-50 minutes**, or until the center is set and a toothpick inserted comes out clean.
6. Allow the pie to cool before serving.

Butternut Squash and Sage Ravioli

Ingredients:

- 1 small butternut squash, peeled, seeded, and cubed
- 1 tbsp olive oil
- Salt and pepper, to taste
- 1 package fresh ravioli (store-bought or homemade)
- 1/4 cup unsalted butter
- 10-12 fresh sage leaves
- 1/4 cup grated Parmesan cheese
- 1 tbsp chopped fresh parsley (optional)

Instructions:

1. Preheat the oven to **400°F (200°C)**.
2. Toss the cubed butternut squash with olive oil, salt, and pepper. Roast for **25-30 minutes** until tender and caramelized.
3. In a food processor, blend the roasted butternut squash until smooth.
4. Cook the ravioli according to package instructions.
5. In a pan, melt the butter over medium heat. Add the sage leaves and cook until crispy, about **1-2 minutes**.
6. Drain the ravioli and toss in the sage butter sauce. Top with Parmesan cheese and fresh parsley. Serve immediately.

Roasted Chicken with Autumn Vegetables

Ingredients:

- 1 whole chicken (about 4 lbs)
- 2 tbsp olive oil
- Salt and pepper, to taste
- 1 tsp dried thyme
- 1 tsp dried rosemary
- 2 cloves garlic, smashed
- 2 carrots, peeled and cut into chunks
- 2 parsnips, peeled and cut into chunks
- 2 sweet potatoes, peeled and cut into chunks
- 1 onion, quartered
- 1 cup chicken broth

Instructions:

1. Preheat the oven to **425°F (220°C)**.
2. Rub the chicken with olive oil, salt, pepper, thyme, rosemary, and garlic.
3. In a roasting pan, arrange the carrots, parsnips, sweet potatoes, and onion. Pour the chicken broth over the vegetables.
4. Place the chicken on top of the vegetables. Roast for **1 1/2 to 2 hours**, or until the chicken is golden brown and the internal temperature reaches **165°F (75°C)**.
5. Let the chicken rest for **10-15 minutes** before carving and serving with the roasted vegetables.

Cranberry Orange Sauce

Ingredients:

- 12 oz fresh cranberries
- 1/2 cup orange juice
- 1/2 cup granulated sugar
- 1/4 cup water
- Zest of 1 orange
- Pinch of salt

Instructions:

1. In a saucepan, combine the cranberries, orange juice, sugar, water, and orange zest.
2. Bring to a boil over medium heat, then reduce to a simmer. Cook for **10-15 minutes**, stirring occasionally, until the cranberries burst and the sauce thickens.
3. Remove from heat and let cool. The sauce will thicken further as it cools.
4. Serve chilled or at room temperature.

Autumn Spice Cake

Ingredients:

- 2 cups all-purpose flour
- 1 1/2 tsp baking powder
- 1/2 tsp baking soda
- 1 1/2 tsp ground cinnamon
- 1/2 tsp ground nutmeg
- 1/4 tsp ground ginger
- 1/4 tsp ground cloves
- 1/2 tsp salt
- 1/2 cup unsalted butter, softened
- 1 cup brown sugar, packed
- 2 large eggs
- 1 cup applesauce
- 1 tsp vanilla extract
- 1/2 cup buttermilk

Instructions:

1. Preheat the oven to **350°F (175°C)**. Grease and flour a 9-inch cake pan.
2. In a bowl, whisk together the flour, baking powder, baking soda, cinnamon, nutmeg, ginger, cloves, and salt.
3. In a separate bowl, cream the butter and brown sugar until light and fluffy.
4. Add the eggs, one at a time, beating well after each addition.

5. Mix in the applesauce and vanilla extract.

6. Gradually add the dry ingredients to the wet ingredients, alternating with the buttermilk. Start and end with the dry ingredients.

7. Pour the batter into the prepared pan and bake for **30-35 minutes**, or until a toothpick inserted into the center comes out clean.

8. Let the cake cool in the pan for 10 minutes before transferring to a wire rack to cool completely.

Butternut Squash Soup with Cream

Ingredients:

- 1 medium butternut squash, peeled, seeded, and cubed
- 1 tbsp olive oil
- 1 medium onion, chopped
- 2 cloves garlic, minced
- 4 cups vegetable broth
- 1/2 tsp ground nutmeg
- 1/2 tsp ground cinnamon
- Salt and pepper, to taste
- 1/2 cup heavy cream

Instructions:

1. Preheat the oven to **400°F (200°C)**.
2. Toss the butternut squash with olive oil, salt, and pepper. Roast for **25-30 minutes** until tender.
3. In a large pot, sauté the onion and garlic over medium heat until softened, about **5 minutes**.
4. Add the roasted squash and vegetable broth to the pot. Bring to a simmer and cook for **10 minutes**.
5. Puree the soup with an immersion blender or in batches using a regular blender until smooth.
6. Stir in the cream, nutmeg, and cinnamon. Adjust seasoning with salt and pepper.
7. Heat through and serve.

Mulled Wine with Spices

Ingredients:

- 1 bottle red wine (750 ml)
- 1/4 cup brandy
- 1/4 cup honey or sugar (to taste)
- 1 orange, sliced
- 2 cinnamon sticks
- 4 cloves
- 2 star anise
- 1/2 tsp ground nutmeg

Instructions:

1. In a large saucepan, combine the wine, brandy, honey, orange slices, cinnamon sticks, cloves, star anise, and nutmeg.
2. Heat over medium-low heat, stirring occasionally, until warmed through (do not boil).
3. Once hot, reduce the heat to low and let it simmer for **15-20 minutes** to allow the flavors to infuse.
4. Strain the mulled wine to remove the spices and orange slices.
5. Serve warm in mugs, garnished with extra orange slices or cinnamon sticks if desired.